Day-Shine

Chong Hyon-jong

Day-Shine

Poems by
Chong Hyon-jong

Translated and introduced by
Wolhee Choe and Peter Fusco

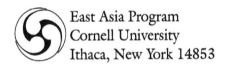

East Asia Program
Cornell University
Ithaca, New York 14853

The Cornell East Asia Series is published by the Cornell University East Asia Program and has no formal affiliation with Cornell University Press. We are a small, non-profit press, publishing reasonably-priced books on a wide variety of scholarly topics relating to East Asia as a service to the academic community and the general public. We accept standing orders which provide for automatic billing and shipping of each title in the series upon publication.

If after review by internal and external readers a manuscript is accepted for publication, it is published on the basis of camera-ready copy provided by the volume author. Each author is thus responsible for any necessary copy-editing and for manuscript formatting. Submission inquiries should be addressed to Editorial Board, East Asia Program, Cornell University, Ithaca, New York 14853-7601.

Publication of this book was supported by a generous grant from the Korean Culture and Arts Foundation.

Photo by Park Young-suk

Number 94 in the Cornell East Asia Series.
© 1998 Wolhee Choe. All rights reserved
ISSN 1050-2955
ISBN 1-885445-94-6 pb
ISBN 1-885445-54-7 hc

13 12 11 10 09 08 07 06 05 04 03 02 01 00   8 7 6 5 4 3 2 1

To Professor Peter H. Lee

Contents

II. Depthless Heart

III. Looking into the Grass

Acknowledgements

Peter H. Lee read the manuscript several times and suggested a great many improvements. We owe special thanks for his care and kindness. Our thanks also go to David McCann, whose appreciation of the poems made the book possible, to Paul Hamill, whose editorial work refined the translations in a number of ways, and to Karen Smith for her reading of the manuscript, unflagging support, and doing all that was necessary to make the book.

We wish to thank the editors of the following journals, where some of these translations first appeared in different versions: *Confrontation, Crab Creek Review, Home Planet News, Earthwise Review, Pennsylvania Review, Touchstone, Translation,* and *Webster Review.*

Finally we thank the Korean Culture and Arts Foundation for its generous grants to undertake the translation and to support the publication of this work.

Introduction

Chong Hyon-jong's poems in this volume are collected from two of his books, *So Little Time to Love* (1991) and *One Blossom* (1993). These poems reside in a primal space created and sustained through the poet's own inventive language. Chong's use of "folk Korean," reminiscent of forgotten vernacular, is fresh and vibrant in its novelty and signals a departure both from traditional poetic diction and from his earlier work. At once conversationally lyrical and colloquially philosophical, these poems command the distinction of their own place in contemporary Korean poetry.

Chong's experimental spirit, in common with other contemporary Korean poets, reflects, among other historical contingencies, the unprecedented linguistic sea change effected by ceaseless political upheavals in Korea in the latter half of the twentieth century. The poet had come of age in the midst of turbulent change, when the Korean peninsula became one of the most dangerous battlegrounds in the world with the constant threat of armed international confrontation. This condition of political volatility, which repeatedly broke apart his social world, persisted throughout his life. With the Second World War, Korea recovered her language and independence from Japanese occupation, and with the Korean armistice in 1953, after the ravages of war that lasted three years, experienced an influx of things American. Then the final fall of the military regime, after a series of increasingly oppressive military dictatorships for three decades, ushered in violent economic changes, dismantling traditional holds on the economy. The fall of the Berlin Wall rekindled an impatient hope for unification of Korea, and the decline of Soviet Russia held forth the promise of a New World. Chong was at his most prolific under the military oppression of the 70s and 80s, and the horror of the regime's inhumanity haunts his poetic personae.

1

Chong's formative years (b. 1939) were marked by an abrupt linguistic shift. During the Japanese occupation of Korea (1912-1945), elementary schools as well as universities allowed students to speak only the Japanese language, and Korean language publications and other normal cultural activities in Korean were suppressed and ceased completely toward the end of the occupation. The surrender of Japan to the Allied Forces in 1945 abruptly ended this situation, and the Korean language was liberated. The poet's schooling therefore began in a state of cultural shake-up, where everything—textbooks and teachers—had to be restructured. This phenomenal upheaval brought about numerous social changes and greatly accelerated the pace of language change. From elementary school to his college years and beyond, Chong lived in an environment that was electric with international and domestic/political changes.

Whether Chong's response to a linguistically open city, Seoul, led the young poet to creative freedom cannot be proven, but it is likely to have given him a special awareness of the reconstructive potential of language. Elementary school teachers in his classes faced children without textbooks and without coherent policies. The U.S. army stationed on the outskirts of Seoul at this time became part of the contemporary Korean landscape, flooding Seoul with English language publications (*Life, Time, Newsweek, Stars and Stripes*). As the newly-established government of Korea jettisoned all Japanese textbooks in primary schools as part of an attempt to wipe out colonial influences, school teachers faced the problem of writing new ones overnight. They met the problem by replacing Japanese educational material with American. In the beginning they adopted the texts wholesale; English primers used in American schools were directly translated into Korean. Later textbooks continued to be modeled after American school texts. The American educational system shifted formal Korean education away from the Germanic system which had been adopted in its Japanese form.

New Influences, New Syntax

The Korean language, the silenced native tongue, awakened from her thirty-three year sleep, met the onslaught of the new English tongue as if a floodgate had been opened upon a fountain. That is to say, elements of the old were mixed with, and sometimes distorted by, the rush of new words and ways of speaking. The change in schools was especially important, because the young poet was required to study English as a second language in middle school. French and German were relegated to third language status, to be taken in high school, while everyone had to take English.

With the sudden influx of new cultural material and the loosening of authoritarian control on language activities, the future poet was placed in an extraordinary situation where experimentation was seductive for someone sensitive to language. Regardless of the official status of various languages and cultures, it is not difficult to imagine the child comparing his spoken Korean at home with written (translated) Korean learned at school, and comparing his native expressions with those of Western languages he heard and learned. Later, as a Korean poet trying to repossess his native language, Chong's uncommon awareness of different sounds, nuances and syntax played an important role in creating his own extraordinary poetic idiom. His early poems are notable for incorporating elements of other languages and literatures.

The new influences were not only linguistic. Chong studied philosophy at Yonsei University at a period when postwar existentialist literature from Europe dominated Korean academic and literary life. After college he worked as a journalist for various newspapers and magazines and then taught Korean literature, a topic that in effect had to be recreated, at the Arts Institute of Seoul and later at Yonsei University. While still developing his style, he spent six months in 1974 at the University of Iowa's International Writers' Program. Given such a background, linkages to various Western literary traditions and philosophies in his poetry would be expected.

For many critics, the experimentation with language based on foreign languages is the distinguishing mark of Chong's early poems. In his early poems a novel syntax has been said to resemble syntactic structures of one or another European language, for example, involving prepositional phrases and relative clause-modifiers, rarely used in Korean syntax. His unconventionally specific or precise use of particles (morphemes that mark grammatical cases in Korean) and lengthy modifiers are also said to be of foreign origin. Through such syntactic experiments, as well as selective adaptation of Western poetic thoughts, the lines of his early poems were rendered fresh and powerful. Unfortunately, the translation into a Western language cannot capture much of this unusualness.

His syntactic experiments are of course inseparable from Chong's appropriation of Western poetic traditions, especially Romanticism and modernism, both of which fit his penchant for philosophical musings. His poetry, selectively embodying ideas and models from Western literature, especially its contemporary manifestations, has forged a fresh path for contemporary Korean poetry.[1]

---

[1] Since a detailed analysis of Chong's imaginative syntax, though interesting in itself, requires a larger space than this introduction, I'd like to direct the interested reader to Kim Hyun's article, "The Poetics of a Drunken Beggar" in his book, *Analysis and Interpretation*, 1988.

The Energy of the Vernacular

The poems in this volume reflect a different, later kind of experimentation. They present the reader with a decisive move away from earlier syntactic experiments with written Korean. In the poems we have translated, the shorter lines contain rhythms and phrases in a powerful vernacular reconstituted from indigenous and almost forgotten idioms. These experiments with the vernacular are as far-reaching and revolutionary as his syntactic experiments. During the Japanese occupation, Korean spoken privately in the family, unlike written Korean for public use, could never be completely controlled or suppressed. Even during the miliary dictatorship, spoken Korean prevailed as a medium of lively and truthful exchange despite oppressive measures curtailing freedom of expression for the press and in academic quarters. Chong has found in the continuing oral tradition of vernacular Korean a fresh source for poetry. Emerging from historical and intellectual contingencies of modern Korean, Chong has penetrated deeply into the world of vernacular expression and found it more universal than the world of written culture. Fossilized idioms are awakened into new life as he incorporates contemporary life in this new work. While he had initially absorbed Western syntax and literary modes into his earlier poems for greater poetic unity, in the second phase of experimentation that I have tried to capture, he creates from the indigenous Korean past an all-inclusive vision of human reality.

One work will serve as an example. The word "darkness" in "In Praise of Dusk" is transformed from a simple idea in the contemporary vernacular to a cosmic perception. The notion of darkness, purged of its conventional connotations of fear, despair, and ignorance, gets a new life of plenitude and luxury in this poem. Darkness is linked with common and overused expressions like *pungbuhaejinda* (becoming abundant) and *kipkokipta* (deeply deep). No longer clichés, these terms are both the agents and objects of transformation when they are ways of encountering the infinite, the void, the world without distinction.

> . . .
> In the deepest recesses of the dark,
> there's nothing not mutually touching;
> nor is there distinction
> (to be opulent is to lack distinction).
> My body is surpassingly open,
> like the void;
> there's nothing my hands cannot touch.
> Water is the same:
>
> its hands extend to infinity— (24)

4

This poem which begins "With the passing of twilight" redeems the darkness with "there's nothing not mutually touching," where hands touch infinity.

The poems in this collection make it clear that Chong's inventive vernacularity does not disown his earlier embrace of Western literature, nor does it simply reinstate a "return to nature" of the Eastern kind. A breath of the new touches us with a recognition of both. Chong's 1985 collection of poems, *The Beggar and the Madman*, has a short poem "In Praise of Dusk" which dispossesses art itself to acknowledge poetry beyond the power of words: "the silence of the naturally silent/ the beauty of the naturally beautiful." These words assert a visionary world of poetic unity beyond the divisions made by words, an affirmation that is common to both traditions. The unity he seeks is the process of unifying, a Romantic notion and, at the same time, a much more comprehensive whole that suggests an ongoing appropriation whose end is "0" (110). Approached as Eastern, the poetry offers Laotzuan cosmos, but its unity is subject to skepticism, for the poet desires to transcend radical doubts about the condition of human existence and knowledge.[2] Because of this skeptical probing, Chong's sensuous energy and pervasive sorrow appear at times closer to the Romantic spirit than to Eastern philosophical equanimity. While such lines as "Come to the empty site of my mind/ Run, play, or sleep/ as your pleasure dictates" ("Unless the Mind is Dispossessed," *B&M*, 100) sound the note of peace, others like "Certain Sorrow" (28) send a melancholic echo that may remind us of Coleridge.

> At dawn,
> at the cusp of sleep,
> anew, once more, again,
> a certain sorrow spreads
> soaking up the blindness of life,
> expanding interminably.
>
> I want to see grasshoppers.

The same melancholy in "Sorrow" (32) offers a reverberation of late Yeats.

> I have ambled the earth.
> I have encountered people.

[2] Stanley Carvell, "In Quest of the Ordinary: Texts of Recovery," *Romanticism and Contemporary Criticism*, 1986, 187.

What alone persists
is sadness.

Anesthetized and electrified expressions,
guarded and unlocked gesticulations, and
desires which only depletion can arrest
have I encountered.

Only sorrow is eternal.

The simultaneously emptied and plentiful state of his poetry suggests the
Yeatsean Romantic desire to rescue the moment from time (*The Collected
Poems of W. B. Yeats,* 1976, 263). This Romantic desire to live in the mo-
ment and the regret at failing to do so may bring about a Buddhist reflection
as in "So Little Time to Love" (25). The speaker realizes and regrets that
each moment has not been made into "a budding rose full blown." Thus the
fully-lived moment alludes not only to Romantic transcendental desire but
to the Buddhist notion of the moment of sufficiency and plenitude—the uni-
versal totality. Through juxtapositions such as those of Romantic and Bud-
dhist sensibilities his poetry becomes free of Romantic despair of the impos-
sibility of living in the moment. This freedom may be the crux of his dis-
tinctly contemporary sensibility; the body appears as the most frequent meta-
phor for transcendence. The heavy body lifting itself thereby "renders itself/
just wind" (109). Like the drunkenness he sings of, the spirit (freedom) is of
the body in pleasure and sorrow. In addition, it may be that the Romantic
threads that enter into his poetry weave transcendence of our time because
Eastern thoughts have surfaced from a visionary core. Chong's vernacular
diction and his physicality are complimentary. They have the power to reach
us directly as if from life itself, even as they reflect his poetic artifice which
is both Romantic and Eastern.

Nature and Humanity

Chong's reconstruction of Romantic moments suggests a Taoist meta-
morphosis into forms of nature, where the poetic consciousness is so nimble
as to become bodily a bubble, cloud, wind, tree, etc., as in numerous poems
grouped in Section III of the present collection. In particular, this is true in
poems like "Calf" (16), "Upon Arriving at Lake Maeji" (102), and "While
Blanketing the Earth—I am Ant" (105).

With the surface of the lake
I likewise ripple out.
Look, a mind
uncircumscribed. (102)

If the poet's mind is like "a freshly emptied receptacle" ready to receive
"common humanity" as Yu Pyungken remarked,[3] how does "common
humanity" make its presence known in his poems? It appears that the
receptacle itself is Chong's "common humanity," and what is his recep-
tacle but his poetic language? Here we face the same problem of de-
scribing Chong's poetic voice, though from a different angle, with which
we began this introduction. Just as we have attempted to understand his
unique poetic language by examining the recent history of the Korean
experience of language, we can look into the structures of the Korean
language to understand Chong's poetic mind as a receptacle of shared
humanity.

The reader will readily note that even the most intensely lyrical of
Chong's poems have a strange distancing effect, as if to make room for that
"common humanity" that surrounds the speaker like a halo. Although our
translations can present only a dim glow of the original halo, it may not be
possible to express what we, as readers, saw and felt as we read and reread
these poems. The Korean language itself is at play, especially its tendency
to generalize, or to collectivize, by allowing the grammatical subject to
remain in the background. The result is a sense of philosophical distance.
Chong's perceptions are often finely detailed yet the language simultaneously
reveals and effaces the persona. The common humanity that the critic iden-
tified emerges in this way from the generalizing tendency of Korean syn-
tax. The same distancing through syntax may appear to diminish lyricism
to some readers, but it offers a range of thought uncommon to lyrical po-
ems. His poem, "Calf" (16), has a wanderer who does not roam leisurely
but is "crazed," and a calf that "frolics," but the reader is engaged in a
discourse on the nature of lived time, as the "crazed" wanderer merges with
the frolicking calf.

> In the fields of Wonsong,
> where I wander
> crazed,

---

[3] "Understanding Poetic Phrases," *Shimsung*, March 1979, 100.

7

a calf
just a month old
frolics about.

Because of you
this world first spun
a month ago.

In the original, the grammatical subject for frolicking is syntactically ambiguous; it could be either the speaker or the calf, or both, so that the calf and "I" become one before the third stanza where the world is one with them. In other poems, when the speaker merges similarly with stars, mirrors, or the sky, entering into the flesh of the brightness or the firmament with a single verb, its resultant eroticism is a mere suggestion, a mere hint that vanishes as soon as it registers as a possibility. This effect comes from Chong's lines being both abstract and lyrical—"common" and personal. Even when Chong describes women's body parts, the reader's perception is quickly freed from the particular to receive that common humanity, as though it too had been freshly emptied. In this way, the sensuous and the abstract achieve an actual bonding grounded in grammar.

Chong's lyrical detachment has earned him the reputation for writing religious or philosophical poems. He may deserve the reputation, but what distinguishes his poetry is his ability to sustain an instinctive level of innocence through which the self becomes cosmic. States of purity indicate a moving away from early forms, from knowledge and scholarship, and a returning to the mother's womb. This poetic evolution is neither psychological nor analytical; it is a returning to childhood, to the rural, to directness of expression, and finally to "nature," as opposed to politics with its greed and nonsense. Reflecting the search for poetry, the poet praises being weak, passive, and empty. To cultivate poetic sensibility is to look betwixt and between, to abide in emptiness, through fasting of the mind to realize it.

In his earlier poems, Chong does not escape Romantic intoxication with death, and his words are, as it were, engulfed in the existential morass. Later his poetry arises from the field of the naked mind free of conceptual divisions and logical oppositions, not leaving behind the initial intoxication but observing it with the equanimity of a Taoist. Tao, identified as nature in his poems, returns to itself: the infinite, continuous, uninterrupted, and constant.[4] The philosophy of returning is the philosophy of "0" (110) or the circle.

---

[4] Witter Bynner, "The Way of Life," *The Works of Witter Bynner: Chinese Translations*, ed. J. Draft. 1982, 349.

. . . whither and whence from there to there
0 is the origin and end
0 is life's portrait
0 is the figuration of presence and absence empty and full
What is 0?
0 is light
the air's breathing
a roll and a game
a halo if donned
0 big and bright
0 is life's looking glass
0 is love
0, the meat of the grain
the flesh of the fruit
. . .

Chong frequently starts from the linguistic ground of Korean folk and popular songs and sayings. Starting out with clichés or near-clichés, he unlocks their mythic meaning. He opens up possibilities of new meaning by novel juxtapositions, parodies, or partial substitutions and changes. Since words, once uttered, begin to limit the reality to be comprehended, he tries to rescue words by lifting them from a given context and placing them in poetic constructions where they may float freed from contentious discursiveness. The avoidance of discursiveness characterizes Chong's "religious and philosophical" poems. Even the lengthy narrative poems in Section II of this collection are far from discursive, as in "You Must Lose to Gain—India Poem III" (70).

. . .
I now understand
(indeed, knowing anything
takes time)
the adage: "As simple as truth."
How drummed into one ear,
it rolled out the other;
and now I dare to coin my own: "If you don't lose,
you don't gain."

You must lose to gain.
. . .

Given the degree to which Chong's inventiveness is specific to Korean syntax and essentially untranslatable, what did the translators hope to accomplish? Alas, hardly any of his playful word games can be conveyed; only the spirit of poetic parallels and reversals. Even though it is beyond our ability to transfer, in translation, Chong's linguistic experiments, we did attempt to capture his poetic embrace of objects, daily language, people, and life itself, as well as his capacity to sustain the human spirit against the ceaseless falls of a perishing world. Chong's moment is that of unity, when the poet's "lucidity asserts." Thus, in "A Thing Called the Body" (101), the body sails "like a boat that goes/ by waterways and fireways." But this body, though it suffer burning or drowning, promises transforming beauty as its perceptual and experiential center: it is "My body, the universe./ My body, the void." Chong's visceral awareness of time, "The life of nervous tissue is the life of time," is reconciled into his spiritual acceptance of things as they are. Whenever possible, the translators have sought to retain the essence of Chong's poetic transformations.

I
The Smell of Earth

Four Seasons for Trees

When in bud,
the brilliant joy and luxuriant surprise of spring
exceed even the glint in a child's eyes
which delights in and is astonished by everything it sees.
Stout hearted in water or fire,
its youth of pale green leaves,
which quiver in this wind or that,
tickles the legs of birds perched on its branches;
then, in season, darkly luscious under the summer sun,
it becomes a woman in her late forties
who tries a heavier rouge.
Already in autumn, as the leaves fall
trees stir from their exuberant summer nap
and with the autumn wind
awake with taciturn time
and opens their inner eyes upon themselves.

Trees on the mountain covered with snow:
oh transparent naked mind!

To Get Attached to Someplace Is Hell*
—May 1980, Kwangju

. . . and the others attain power, and the punishment for their success is quite
like the following: once someone has committed a transgression to gain
power, he uses that power to secure the freedom to commit other crimes.
—part of Maurice Blanchot's explanation of the world of the Marquis de
Sade

> Should you scoop words up
> and throw them away
> and scoop them up again,
> the corpse
> remains unseen.
>
> The corpses seem to be buried
> really deeply,
> more deeply than the heart.

*The title is a parody of a popular Korean song which says that attachment makes a foreign place
home.

14

Self-Deception

Self-deception:
how stunning,
how blameless,
how forthright,
how immutable.
Truly stunning,
blameless,
forthright,
immutable.
Self-deception,
inescapably us.

Calf

In the fields of Wonsong,
where I wander
crazed,

a calf
just a month old
frolics about.

Because of you
this world first spun
a month ago.

Movement, What Beauty, for the Grace of Trees

People amble in this direction under the trees.
Beauty thrives in their movements!
All movement—what beauty
—especially the grace of trees.

In Autumn

(Although every season is just
a spectacle for our eyes)
Look what the autumn does:
its exterior is not its outside
but is its heart.
I cannot see the edge of mind
in the autumn wind so just walk
windward into the heart
of fall.

Walk inside the fall and wonder
why it spreads out edgeless;
why the violated, vacant mind suffers
playing a kid's game: civilization sliding
over the kernels of institutions.
Stepping lightly within the outside,
in the autumn wind I marvel at the leafpiles of mind.

A Lullaby
—At night with insomnia

Sleep
as farmers implant
sweat, heart, a lifetime
all in the soil.

Sleep
since no one disinters
the buried miners
like coal.

Sleep above all else
soaked in the long shadow
of restless ghosts of this land
in its boundless sorrow
that worms its way into your flesh.

The Smell of Earth

When I smell earth,
I'm not alone in this world.

With a dead branch, I dig up the soil in the backyard and sniff it.
The savor of earth! This vigorous aroma touches—what?
The distant source. A living embrace. Breath.

All lives, gathering here floating in its scent, rise and hang
like clusters of potatoes.

The smell of earth.
The conniver of life.

Ubiquitously Pitiful

Ubiquitously pitiful
we humans are, moreover,
parasites
infesting another's wound
sucking blood:
ourselves, likewise,
hosts.

We can only eat
with enthusiasm,
produce blood
with diligence.

The Gossamer Thread of Life

Even if all life long I sang,
my singing could never approach
the pheasant's song
which you hear in the mountains, as if in recollection,
which instantly reveals the abyss in the sea of our lives;
I would never approach
that brawny timbre
which is full of worms and earth and shadow,
full of its own abounding life,
without any training in voice,
without even the mimicry of words.

My song breaths
the all-consuming fires of the physical
life's gossamer.
Words! I want you,
gossamer threads of life.

The Rural Night Bus

Off in the distance appears
the rural night bus.

The lights within it shine.

You can just make out the passengers
within the moving brightness
of the rural night bus.

I want to place this night bus in the sky,
like the brightest of suns.

In Praise of Dusk

With the passing of twilight
the world becomes richer!

Trees drenched in dusk,
buildings of old stone,
shafts from mercury lights in the dimness,
the depth of the dark
framed by the blue-black sky.

In the deepest recesses of the dark,
there's nothing not mutually touching;
nor is there distinction
(to be opulent is to lack distinction).
My body is surpassingly open,
like the void;
there's nothing my hands cannot touch.
Water is the same:

its hands extend to infinity—

So Little Time to Love

There's so little time to love.
A child toots honk! honk! on his plastic reed-pipe.
Scallions in the tied-up bundle of an old aunty
keep on growing through the folds of the bundle.
A grandpa's running after a bus.
Two girls, it's irrelevant why,
promenade with two or three roses in hand.
All buds are unfading!
And the chestnut blossoms are flowering still
in the vinyl satchel that holds some lady's chestnuts;
The blooms are exploding.

Natureward

With a tuft of mouth-watering grass
I entice a grazing goat.
I only want to pet him,
to gaze into his eyes.
By stroking his leathery skin
and peering eye to eye, I revert
to my own nature.
A swelling abundance spills over the rice paddy banks
and ceaselessly, incessantly,
animals draw me along.
Unresisting I am hauled
natureward.

Abundance spills over the rice field.

The Desolate Field

In the sunlight,
in the autumn air,
amidst the ripening rice,
earth and sky are bright,
and yet,
ah! the field is desolate
without grasshoppers!

Oh, this foreboding stillness—
The link of the golden chain of life has snapped . . .

Certain Sorrow

At dawn,
at the cusp of sleep,
anew, once more, again,
a certain sorrow spreads
soaking up the blindness of life,
expanding interminably.

I want to see grasshoppers.

A Certain Handkerchief

What a sad sight
the handkerchief
is
folded
which
the pocket of last year's
old clothes
holds.

Body Movements

If I raise my neck
the sun rolls in and
if I stretch out my arms
the horizon extends
into a far distance.
(I shall not now mention
the sorrow that body movements possess;
I shall not now mention this sorrow,
like a lengthening shadow drizzling on the earth,
except to sing of its tangible intoxication.)
Don't you, when you stretch,
don't you hear
the tingle of the air?
Along the dirt road,
drunk on, and buoyed up, by the resilient earth,
I walk on.
I walk on thinking how dance has no form apart
but when I bounce up
flying the body,
the leap makes gravity
a thread of air,
like grass and trees
hoisting the earth up,
imbibing the elasticity of the earth.

A Choice Landscape

A snow day in late winter:
muted snowflakes in the softening weather.
The footprints of a man and woman led uphill,
the slopes were layered as with a fresh skin.
Exhaling breath clouds all over the valley,
they did it leaning against the chestnut tree.
Spring arriving sooner than usual,
the chestnut tree stood flabbergasted
having unfolded in one afternoon
all the buds set to flower in the days to come.

Sorrow

1

I have ambled the earth.
I have encountered people.
What alone persists
is sadness.

2

Anesthetized and electrified expressions,
guarded and unlocked gesticulations, and
desires which only depletion can arrest
have I encountered.

Only sorrow is eternal.

Day-Shine

Day-shine,
persimmons on a tree:
innumerable flame flowers
have lit up
heaven and earth.
Yet if these sunbeams
and that daylight
all add up,
shall they glow as brightly?
The persimmons still remain unpicked
after first frost and winter coming.
Copious,
crows and magpies in surfeit,
heaven and earth in satiety.
My mind also over there
speeds to the persimmon tree
and opens up.

Sleep-Talking

Sleep-talking:
too profound,
too distressing
and utterly
petrifying.

Water Sounds

In a ravine,
the water's din,
words liquidated;
the water's din,
my tongue
wafted.

Had I Known Each Instant Was a Flower in Bud

Sometimes I regret:
that occasion, that affair
might have been a gold mine . . .
That moment, that person,
that time, that object
might have been a gold mine.
Had I delved deeper,
spoken more,
listened harder,
loved more.

Was I half-mute,
hard of hearing, perhaps,
and dumb?
That moment when,
had I loved more . . .

Had I known
each instant was a flower in bud,
that could have blossomed
under my ardor.

Enclasped

Like a tree
in the rain
out there, anywhere,
I want to be nestled.
Where is the rain
Where is the tree
Where is the embrace?

Art!

—To Mikail Baryshinikov

Your dancing, your face
have wrung me out
like laundry. The wash
water is dripping.

Outside the theater.
lest my stepping on the ground
disfigure the things around,
lest I tread down them . . .
I walk cautiously, as if treading in air.
Perfect poise on the point of emerging
extends between the quotidian
nexus of things
and a counterpoint in the spirit. The wounded mind
scatters a sheen, like pearls gathered into a dozen baskets,
peers through a shimmering nimbus,
as if the sun permeated it.

The sky is
the pupil of the eye, the earth
the sole of the foot.
Art!
The winged flesh
of innocence and love.

In the Forest

1

Handsomest of all creation,
you, tree,
my mind and heart are now
also green
where large and small capillaries
are a fountain of bird songs
a nest of wings
(twittering blood veins
flying arteries).

2

My lifelong dream has been
to bed a woman among the birds
and sire fledged above and human below
a half-bird, half-human child.
Bird, my magic spell.
Tree, my amulet.

II
Depthless Heart

Depthless Heart
—October 1974 in Iowa

October night in Iowa City. After the Finnish-American poet, Anselm Hollo, reads his poetry, we, Anselm, Katarina, some novelist and a woman who was perhaps his lover, and I, enter a bar.

Katarina, a Greek poet, asks me what the population of Seoul is. About seven million, I reply, but I don't know how many have died. Katarina laughs heartily, and we drink elbow to elbow.

> What is this something better than wings,
> the mind, simply the air.
> Freedom?
> Oh, this field-like
> self as is,
> unprocessed
> sensation of the real object!
> The mind?
> Well, try touching it.
> I say touch it.
> Please touch it.

Quitting the bar into the cool breeze and the starry night sky, Anselm says to me pointing far away, "Do you see the fence over there? That's the police station." "We can't see within, but it's probably made so they can see without," says I. Something's excited me.

We move to a cafe and drink three cups of what's called an Irish Coffee.

The ride home in a car driven by the novelist,
three a.m.,
I got out in front of the apartment I was staying at.
Anselm followed suit,
and we embraced. I've never
experienced such a hug,
a heart
embracing the globe.

Eating a White Radish

In the radish fields of Chonggye,
I've been given a fine-looking radish,
the kind we would use for winter pickling.
While crossing the hill,
I'm eating it in earnest.
(Although I've eaten enough of it to grate my stomach
how could I have known how intense my munching really was?)
My companion
explains grinning at me:
"You have been chomping away on the radish, clutching it tightly
    against your chest."
That's when I realize what I have been doing.

Aha! In my childhood I used to eat these succulent radishes
picked from the fields at home.
I lift the radish I have been eating up high
and speak in the tongue of my intestines
spellbound by memory:
"This radish I am eating is my childhood!"

In Haktong Village

1

I enter the village at night
lighting the pitch dark night with a flashlight.
(A night in the country!
How long has it been since I came here?)
Ghosts wrap around my body,
ghosts whose whereabouts I have puzzled over
since electricity was installed into country corners.

The hometown abode of my companion, Pyongjae Kosa,*
who just walked out of an elementary school textbook,
whose life-long dream is to play the flute on a cow's back;
and another companion, Kisim Kosa,
who still dreams of stepping on the shadows
of the morning glory in bloom after it has climbed up to the
    windows
of the childhood country house,
to hide and spread
the world, the sun, the moon
opened within their shapes and fragrances.
With these two companions I am treading the village path
intoxicated even before setting out
on the home-made wine I haven't even drunk
and licking the wind with a tongue
elongated five feet
with the yearning to drink.

2

(Although all the houses on earth are holy)
How immaculate this is
the country house revealed in the morning sunlight!
You still have the shyness nesting within.
How long has it been since I washed my face
in the basin out back in the garden!
I let my sense of touch
now become one with the morning air,
glide endlessly on;
my lungs which have been stationed in the air
now expand into the sky
exhibiting the blue capillaries.

The houses built
of blue air and sunlight.
My lungs are bellowing there
incessant in the atmosphere.

*Kosa: an honorific bestowed on scholar-artists who live away from social rewards.

Empty Room

1

Before it gets cold
I've decided to wallpaper
the vestibule ceiling, kitchen walls, and three rooms;
cost of labor and material totals 250,000 won.
The workers say I only have to provide them with a snack.
Counting is splendid
(though there are exceptions)
since everybody counts.
On this very point
people compete
to deplore accounting.

2

I take all the books out
stacking them on the floor of the verandah
like a pile of fire wood,
like a castle wall,
like a ruin.

The room is utterly emptied out . . . oh! oh!
I am entirely filled.
Oh how wonderful!
(I can't help it if this sounds explanatory)
Oh how wonderful!

Toward the emptied bookcases I
am dancing spontaneously.
Toward the emptied shelves
opening my arms,
embracing the evacuated
Whence is this explosive rapture
embracing the evacuated?

I'm looking at the emptied room
with eyes overflowing
the night deeper than within the books
the empty room.

3

Oh! Oh! I must go where there are no books.
Show by opening my hands, instead of a book,
show my face,
show my eyes,
or my chest or backside;
show the leaves,
earth or sky,
just raw vitality: breath,
blood and semen.

4

Everything vacant is an umbilical cord.
Even if, by mixing books, religion and sex,
you explode, you can not reach
this cosmic breath—
new human beings
who do not support the weight of this land's memory,*
face, blood and an intestinal breath.

5

Human liberation?
We must be liberated from books.
We must be freed from words.
There is no emancipation from this book to another book.
There is no deliverance from this word to that word.
At any rate,
as for the tongue,
it's most useful to kiss with!
Let me say something worth doing:
my blood,
my flesh, my bone,
I must blow this flower up.

*The French poet, St. John Perse, in his "Anabasis" wrote this line: "the men who do not support the weight of this land's memories."

Though Walking Again Today
—A back alley of history

1

Blood this.
This the river.

Phantasy that.
That the cliff.

Blood dripping from the moon,
the blood dried by the sun.

All night long I have chewed upon
six million dried squid.
Arrgh!, the blood from these squid.

2

How has our time presented itself?
Like a banal ambush
drooling without restraint over sacrifices,
going far beyond melodrama,
sinking rather than progressing,
perpetually pacing in place:
enduring as a nightmare.

3

I am sending a gift into that time
after five Korean millennia, capital headlines there

Hippos Herd in the Han River!

Creative Writing 101: Poetry

My own words, on occasion, may be of some use,
but better by far
than the words we've been trained to
is to listen to the live, keen voice
of flowers blooming or a man dying;
better a running leap.
To fall and bleed in the attempt
is even better.
Although the word "view" apparently
opens up vistas, better yet
climb a tree and view the world.
Indeed, grip a live fish
—more alive than any living, moving thing—
rather than hesitate faltering.
Better to grasp fresh confusion,
raid the melon patch at dead of night;
better to snare a sleeping bird
and feel its warm heart beating
in your palm.
These are the world's profundities.
Rather than gape at the teacher's face,
kiss your lover,
look at the blue sky,
dissolve in action
or become expansive, pliant blue air
and rattle the classroom windows
or spread out blue in the sky.

At any rate, be a man
but a man of no use:
Chuang Tsu's: "Ignore
the use of the useless."
The usefulness of the useless!
At least walk with the gait of
the uselessly engaged,
becoming your own self, which recalls
everyone else as
inevitable love-sparks,
inevitable sorrow-sparks,
laughter sparks head-over-heels.
Thus at your touch
flower blood fish melon and bird lover and blue sky
bloom from your flesh and navigate your blood,
the body bruised and the breath uplifted
skyward birthed from the body you love
and outspread over the world.
Let it hover.

Like a Ghost

How I live like a ghost.
The hand grenade which shattered the window
explodes instantly,
turning the building into a gas chamber;
within
with eyes tearing and nose running
unable to see,
unable to breathe,
losing consciousness and on the point of death,
really, how I live like a ghost,
a ghost of rice cake,
a ghost of cow?*
"Hey, scoundrels, aren't you overdoing it?"
(What I'm trying to say is, instead of preventing the students from
going out into the streets of Seoul, why do you shoot so much and tear
the school up into shreds? How come you shoot into the buildings
what's so poisonous it can not be exported? How come you act so
without restraint?)
"We live like worms."
A ghost of worm.
One teacher bleeds from the neck;
another develops shortness of breath from pulmonary infections.
Another, having blown his nose three hundred sixty days,
develops allergies, which create a bloody nose.
Another throws up everything he eats.

Skin afflictions, nose disorders.
Nose frayed, neck frayed, lungs frayed.
Chronic shortness of breath.
All try x-rays.
Indeed even the ghosts bemoan us our lives.
It's hell to get attached to someplace.
It's not someone else's foot;
    after all, it's mine.
    It's not someone else's life;
    after all, it's mine.

This spring
I cannot hear bird song.
Where have all the bumpkin pheasants gone?
Have the magpies all taken flight too?
The campus and the magpies' nests are equally deserted.

The background is marvelous
The background of polite greeting
The background of running away
The background of survival
The background of rice cake
The background of worms
luxuriant smile
smiling like a ghost
free extension and contraction.
This must be a ghost
I shall go on living this way.
How much is this baked mix?
How much is the rice medley?
Slowly, little by little,
really you are killing me.
Really, I go on like a ghost.
—It's hell to get attached to someplace.

*Refers to the most tenacious quality in things.

Dilemma 2

Some "conscience"
drives other minds
into a dilemma.

"Conscience" is lonely;
yet the other minds
like a group wedding
are also lonely.

Everything driven into a dilemma
is lonely.

"Conscience" is cruel.

What makes
"conscience"
and the other minds lonely?
What herds
us all
into a cruel dilemma?

Does the world do it?
Or power?
Does heaven?
Or someone?
Food?
Sex?

Or reality?
Dreams?
What is it?
Our very selves?

Wonderful!
We ourselves,
fleeing a dilemma
and living a dilemma,
head for a dilemma.

Country School House

Oh, the country school house,
the bird's eye view of it
cradles me.
I'm embraced
in its heart.

(Here alone
in the whole wide world
exists)

hallowed peace

time's blossom

echoes of dreams

unblushingly bared cleanliness

the divine exact of the universe.

The exhalations of the living cosmos,
denser than all the shimmering aureoles
of the world's dense forests
encapsulated into a pea-sized pastille.

(How shall my words,
even if meticulously plucked,
brush cheek to cheek
the air's nebulous breath?)

Oh, country school house.

Rice
—Autumn 1985

To see the fully-ripened rice blades
submerged and spoiled in an unexpected autumn flood
hurts.
You people shouldn't talk about a bountiful harvest,
looking at unripened stalks
(Perhaps we should consider it lucky they didn't advertise
    bounteous harvests even before the initial
    replanting of the seedlings).
Concerning the cultivation of rice,
one shouldn't talk about an abundant harvest,
not when the rice stalks stand in the paddies,
not even after harvesting and storing them in the warehouses,
not even after pouring rice in storage jugs at home.
A good harvest is something you can talk about
only when the grains have been cooked
and you stuff them in your mouth.

This story is not restricted to the cultivation of rice.
All the blather about
politics, economics, culture, and education—
all of this is far from the cooked rice in your mouth
but more like face powder,
the cosmetic residue of rice
we harvested this bountiful year.

Intermission
—At night in college town (Shinch'on)

1

As the night turns opaque,
drinkers flood the summer streets.
The fluid energy of alcohol, spilling like phosphorescence,
inflates the earth and the sky.
Even my rotten bones
must have been phosphorescent,
for suddenly two girls dressed in shades of night
charge at me shouting: "Look, Sir!
Sir, see that man. He keeps following us!"
I behold the man, tornado-like, awhirl,
a student who writes verses well
to put it simply.
Since I recognize him,
I face both girls and roar:
"You chicks, I would follow you two too."

(. . . that fellow
might be half the ghost of the departed soul of Samuel Beckett,
    infamous for his pursuit of women)

2

Without even trying to turn back,
I see echoes of reflections of movement,
as though the whole air were a retina
flickering faintly and resounding in my ears.

As to My Inertia
—A shadow of the dead

I am inert by nature . . .
A likely story, say you?
You may be right, but I
seem naturally inert.
Naturally?
If by nature, why?

It has something to do with sorrow.
Sorrow?
And the pain as large as . . .
As large as?
That people die without reason or rhyme
makes me want to kick, to kick a chunk of iron.
That mortal strokes have crippled—oh so many—
makes me want to twist my limbs into braids.
Birds fly,
flowers continue to bloom, and
my body aches.
The dead are not here . . .
With innards disposed to rot,
under the shadow of restless ghosts,
which stretches endlessly
I drink,
entirely
inert . . .

A Fresh Laid Egg

After my hike down the mountain, a young man
at the noodle shop I frequent in summer
presents to me in the beaming sunlight, palm
to palm, what he says is a fresh-laid egg.

May I accept this gift in kind!—
With the warm egg
clutched
and my mind astir in eddies, I descend.
With the new laid egg,
the warmth,
the hallowed stirrings of life,
I who hold the universe in my hand—
I am made glorious!
Never before has the earth
buoyed up my footsteps.

The Death God of Civilization

On the paved road of the apartment village
a chicken struts.
I saw it the day before yesterday.
Again I saw it today.
Chicken
on the paved road,
pathetic, to be sure—
chicken
on the
paved road—
isn't something askew?
Life,
aha!
Life,
aha!—all told,
isn't it distasteful?
After the frenzied
epileptic fit,
the foaming universe
falls.
Ah!, where has the soil disappeared to?
Where are the worms and creeping things;
where are the streams, and where,
oh where are the rest of the chickens?
Too well-received, too—chicken
on the paved road!—ludicrous.

In this city smothered in the black tar
of progress toward death, what,
chicken, do you peck for?
Since the flowers that bloom on graves
are flowers still,
dark chicken, life's blossom,
what do you peck at?
Perhaps at a purring car?
Or carbon monoxide?
Noise pollution?
We no longer sustain hearts
or the wriggling life
you can peck at.
Blood, red-fresh, alive,
and sprinkled all over,
a mind no longer exists as true as that
to be pecked for,
flightless bird,
bringer of ruin who scampers insanely,
death god of civilization.

To Poverty
—India Poem I

Unable to comfort the poor, Sakyamuni
went himself in rags.
Not politics, nor economics, nor any system,
much less would nation status manage it;
for poverty on earth is eternal.
Concerned about its obdurateness
and perplexed by the unassuageably poor,
he dressed himself in tatters:

through which the nakedness of one man shone
and the eternal homeland of the mind.

It's Not Going Anywhere
—India Poem II

At dusk
a heifer
walks the streets of Bopal.
(What a face!)
The look that doesn't seem to be going anywhere at all,
not going somewhere at all, that look
(it really drives me up a wall)
of not going anywhere at all,
of going nowhere . . .

You Must Lose To Gain
—India Poem III

(I scribble this
having lost something
after spending the evening
with a Danish Poet
who lost something too.)

I now understand
(indeed, knowing anything
takes time)
the adage: "As simple as truth."
How drummed into one ear,
it rolled out the other;
and now I dare to coin my own: "If you don't lose,
you don't gain."

You must lose to gain.

Hands
—*India Poem IV*

Bolt upright, an Indian balladeer sings classical Indian songs. Look how his hands behave: as if pursuing the fragrance of invisible blossoms; as if trying to grasp the unsnatchable blossoms; as if lifting up water; as if stroking a woman's torso.

Our hands.

A Dream Like a Tree

Why abandon a dream! I dream these days
of erecting a home with many rooms,
where I can board and bed waifs and rakes,
pretty deviants and pretty prisoners,
pedestrians stepping backwards, sleepers erect,
seers peering with closed eyes, listeners heeding with their bodies
whose limbs stretch like licorice sticks,
wanderers with their feet swathed in horizons,
non-drivers of cars,
primitives,
stutterers,
slow-pokes,
star-gazers,
in any event, to board and bed those who lack fierceness
to construct for them a many chambered house.
No, not a hotel, not a prison,
neither a hospital nor a school,
just a "local": the whole house abloom
in an exquisite balance of anarchic sensibility.
I'll let no one in without a smatter of self-knowledge;
and none of the interminably unafflicted, no matter what.
No access for strangers to sorrow, of course not;
none for the suffocatingly pig-headed
or the multifarious bloodsuckers;
nor for the uncomprehending (because incomprehensible?) virile
    protozoa:

(I won't allow those scribbling inkblots with their unquestionably
    unassailable infallibility in either).
Parrots are banned, to be sure;
all war-mongers, weapons-dealers, all;
any in love with the nuclear zap—of course not!
And once more, though undoubtedly there are more,
all the rest are excluded.
I leave out those remaining
Yet those who renovate selfhood are welcome whenever.
The pleasure of excluding another is of pleasures the most abject.

Why abandon a dream! My dream these days
is a tree
in whose shadow I breath easy.

Unpaved Depth

When it was a dirt road,
the path uphill had a depth all its own.
That's gone
now it's paved.

The forest sylphs have vanished too.

Deep soil;
shallow asphalt.

Animal accommodations;
human discomfort.

Profound nature;
superficial civilization.

What Are You Looking At?

In the city of Bophal, India,
you, wide open eyes,
what are you looking at?
You, seemingly perfect but blind eyes
of a girl whose face looks plastic,
blinded to death
by Union Carbide gas
and just being buried:
are looking at the sun?
When your eyes touch
the sun, perfect
fading white becomes blind.
When your eyes touch
the light, perfect
is blind. All eyes presumed
perfect are blind.
Your eyes torture,
your eyes faint.
Your eyes vomit, and what are you looking at?
Your eyes!

Blossom

In the corridor
I discerned the excessively beautiful legs of a woman,
and walking down the hill, I thought of them.
A colleague climbing uphill remarked in a voice
athletic and assured:
"Absorbed in poetic thought . . ."
Passing him, I beamed
and mused on:
Aha, good guess! His remark and her legs!
We live in the scintillating flesh,
the ambling window through which
we view the primordial,
the vortex of energy that
swells with the heave of a bellows,
and makes the flesh bloom.
I feel a poem coming on! I have a blossom.

A Certain Peace

In a mountain village in the afternoon, a child almost five years old sits gazing at a ruminating cow. He's oblivious to anyone's approach. Then lifting up his eyes, he brusquely asks me where I live. "I live in Seoul. Do you live here?" Instantly responsive to my voice and feeling safe under the sun, the boy continues staring at the cow. As I gather tufts of straw to feed the beast, the child utters in a cozy tone, "That's what it loves to eat!" I hear familiarity and joy in that voice (for he sees a stranger do what he does.)

I frequently recall the image: "Child Gazing at a Ruminating Cow. An unforgettable picture. Unfading flower. Peace . . .

Portrait of a Youth

A young man loads iron pipes onto a truck. His face inclines as if it were himself he's hoisting. What's exacted? Salvation. Absolute concentration in an instant. The gravity of pipes, pipes pulling the youth down, pipes sucking his everything, that illuminates. The unquenchable limelight. The young man's face contains it all: the lush life, the flush immobility, salvation.

Obscenity

In a full length dream
I am watching porno
where the poses, unexceptional
like in real life, squirm. Then
a novelist of my acquaintance
who walked into the screen
struts out with
a grin of satisfaction.
I continue
anxious. I need to go
somewhere, but time outpaces me.
When should the scene have occurred
for me to enter the shop
to have my watch fixed? Unclear.
The broken watch is unrepaired.
Yes, this is porno.
The streets extend in solemn brutality
road-blocked in all directions.
Arduously crawling
over a crosswalk, conspicuous
even in dreams, and passing
a bookstore, I am being
shaken awake: rise and shine,
and why aren't you ready for work yet?

What is more lurid
than a husband and wife
—the obscenity of institutions,
of legitimacy, of habit,
the security of hackwork,
the chef d'oeuvre of love?
Yes, yes, off to work,
and even worse, to school. So many!
Vulgar as thread-bare hope,
and that hope as denuded as aged despair.
So abstract!—real bodies
and their various posturings
attempting to hatch and try again
the brooding boredom . . .

Enthusiasm

In a side street I haunt
a noodle shop is opened.
In the dimmed evening
under the neon glow
through the window I can make out
the proprietress's rapid movements
in a bright glow.
Oh the excitement of new beginnings,
the brightest spot in the world!
Even the magnolia about to bloom
against a fenced-off neighbor's house
lifts this owner of a new enthusiasm
upward, just skyward, just!

Commodities: Gods of the Material and Opium

1

Commodities are divinities of the material and opium;
department stores are ships sailing for utopia.
Commodities shine, smile sweetly and cozily.
Only satisfaction and pleasure here.
Nerves are calmed; the mind remote.

(Do you feel empty? Embrace commodities.
Anxious? Worship merchandise.
Lonely? Find solace in stores.)

2

This is the temple of Countess Mara.
This is the Church of gold, silver, and precious jewels.
It's a Buddhist shrine with four-wheel drive.

Me, the leather bag, my two arms rising,
Hooray! Fold our wings.
Hooray! Gold and silver salvation.
Hooray! Temple on wheels.

To Cheju Island*

Cheju Island, why don't you
float away forever
wherever far away
faraway from the North
far-off from the South too

far, far and away
to land
      with
           no nation
to land
      of
           no nation

very faraway
far, far and away

*This island province of South Korea is located at the southernmost tip of the country, farthest
from the mainland, Korean Peninsula.

III
Looking into the Grass

When I See a Hole in a Wall

My heart rejoices when I see a hole in a wall;
in fact, it puts me on top of the world.
My erotic glance penetrates this labor
of squirrels or children and I,
solitary, exultantly smile.
A hole hollowed out of a wall or a wrought iron fence
can only exude an uncommon flavor.
Through this hole,
the toil of squirrels or children—does it matter?—
flows an ecstasy akin to finding salvation;
flows an atmosphere which renders divine sanctions inane.
Oh ho!
I shall generate holes in all walls
with the squirrels,
with the children.

In Front of a Glass of Wine

In front of a glass of wine,
which teaches me how to breathe,
in accordance with getting drunk
by emptying,

I drink today.
My body floats around many worlds
and my words echo without a source.
Without politics we'd be unimpeded.

Today, again, I drink
in accordance with getting drunk
by emptying.

Movement Initiated
—In last night's dream

A study. From among the illustrated tomes arranged by disciplines I take a volume, thick as nature herself, shelved among Flora.

An insect contained therein (possibly as a photo-illustration) takes flight, resurrected from where he had expired, and, while stirring back and forth among the flowers, shifts pollen.

(The god of procreation, of production, commences working.)

My eyes, even after awakening, still see with clarity the grinning movement, by which creation thrusts, presses itself out of closed space.

I Have Jumped off the Sun

Watching them sprout
and bloom, and my own tumescence
up and out with no letup,
I have jumped off the sun.
Off the sun
I leapt
(joy of life!)
driving the breeze upon the moon to sail it,
driving the breeze upon the Earth in turn,
and poised on its coiled spring, I grinned.

One task left:
to leap into flowers:
and there
extract the sun from them,
fragrant, red and green.

All <In-between> Is Pitiful

Nothing's more frightening
than the grimace between sleep and awakening;
nothing's more pitiful
than those features.
All <in-between> is frightening.
All <in between> is pitiful.

With This Key

Outside I chance
upon a house key.
Whose is it?
Its ambiguous utility
(all . . . keys . . . track . . .
some . . . fortune . . . keys . . . lock us in . . .)

To tell you the truth
I want this key to
unlock a tree
unlock a ladder
perhaps a river.
With this key I want to unclose
our stark human nakedness
the divestments of time
a footpath
even a field
(Can you see what hand unlocks the field?)
the empty spaces . . .

Leaning on Birds

1

When the birds nest in the sky,
I nest in their wings.
When the birds pipe in the tree tops,
I relocate air and sunlight
into the droplets of bird song.

2

It's not an especially difficult job for me,
this congenital habit.
But when I admire the birds
darting from this tree to that,
I sigh. My own stirrings stall
as the birds flit from tree to tree.

3

Obviously, like birds,
when the total self is in motion,
it alleviates burden and wound.
What, then, can be better than flight
that moves with the mind?

In Praise of Thunder

How, on a summer day,
without the thunderbolt
which cracks the backbone of heaven and earth
how can a man
cleanse himself
body and soul,
really scrub and cool himself
—light as air
to shift like a breeze
let the dawn inundate him?

Thunder,
the umbilical cord of your voice makes us
smile like fresh born babies.
Nothing earthbound has ever given us
the limpid blood
and ambrosia of your voice.
Nothing on earth,
no idea or book,
no triumphs or enchantments,
petty or majestic,
can halt the birth of a world
which your vocal chords bless
as you tongue the cosmic entrails clean;
nor excuse the lucent pathlessness
of your passage.

Thunder, hear me.
The thunder that claps and ceases
between my skull and ribs
is unlike you. It cannot flow through heaven and earth
fearless of beginning or ending, and yet
stops this repetition that digs its own grave,
purging this fetid system,
and burning off the lukewarm, hesitant motion.
I feel as cascading enthusiasm, the measure of which
is the eyes infused with grape green juice
of a young coed who yesterday
in a voice, like seeds floating downslope
wondering if she should root there,
asked: "How's it going, professor?"

Whatever. With you, the ever-dangerous truth,
the nakedness that competes with death
in the fever of my flesh, my poetic alchemy quickens.
Flow on, thunder, as the theme
of my song, my life,
the impure mix,
you, thundering nirvana
you who thunders to the wild joy of kesa.*

Your voice has echoed within.
Look. This new born babe,
thunder-naked, nourishing in
the limpid blood and food
of your voice, relishes
stepping bewitched upon
the luminous pathlessness. Thunderbolt . . .

*A Buddhist term referring to the state of suffering caused by stupidity, hatred, and greed.

Who Can You Be

At the sight of you, I feel
inebriated blood and expectation,
sexual fragrance, shimmering air.
How strange!
I have no worries.
Who can you be?

You blow in the wind
along the dusty roads we take,
into our hearts, at our heels;
you swim before us,
you blow in the wind,
an overflowing presence.
Who can you be?

(To want acquittal in the name of an institution
is obscene; to delude oneself
in the name of convention is obscene.)
Behold nature,
that rippling absence of mind,
INNOCENCE.
You are an overflowing presence:
Who can you be?

Yardstick

A bird is a flying yardstick.
A tree is a standing yardstick.
A fish is a swimming yardstick.
Indeed, is there anything in the world
which is not a yardstick?
A worm is a crawling yardstick.
Animals are furry yardsticks
Water is a flowing yardstick.
Not knowing that they are yardsticks
makes them all better yardsticks.
Man-made artifacts can not be yardsticks.
(Everyone uses artifacts
and claims he is measuring.)
Only nature gets to be yardsticks.
Oh humans, if you are part of nature,
measure the affairs of men!

The Cloud I Lost

The cloud I lost
Is floating in the sky.

The Bee Sting

Propped on a ladder, I was picking apples
with the crazy thrill
of a first time.

On the top branch the ripest
baited my hand.
The instant I clutched the apple, ah!
pain struck.
A bee had stung my finger.
(It was lodged in a breach in the overripe flesh.)
The finger ached more
as time passed.
(To extract a mere lesson
from this incident is patently insipid.)
Although I could not soothe the throbbing pain, my mind
cascaded like an overladen apple tree.
Pain is also the path connecting me with all things in
    the universe;
through a minute injection of venom, my body
merged with nature in its abyss
of vastness.

As Autumn Leaves

Things of life
are like sprouts,
things of life
are like falling leaves
betwixt and between.
I mix blood
with flowing water,
step out on up into the clouds,
lightning in my eyes, wind in my ears.
I dress my flesh in a woman's body,
in all other bodies, like an illumination.

We come and go
back and forth from distance to distance
until we hang like autumn leaves
upon a branch.

A Thing Called the Body

A body measures ninety thousand leagues
or inches and feet.
It can be bathed clean
or purified with exertion—
a jet of ecstasy
a sack of desperation
nine luminous openings
the hub of all
that traffic in and out of its junctions
which penetrate heaven and earth.
In daylight it reflects everything
and at night incarcerates within itself.
Any morning it may be lifted up
or knocked down.
If a fleck of dust makes it cry,
a blade of grass makes it smile.
It's winsome when bouncing up
but also when falling down.
Like earth;
like wine, within which
water and fire dwell
(to get drunk means not segregating water and fire);
like a boat that goes
by waterways and fireways.
Although drowned or burned now and then
the body is purified to eternity.

My body, the universe.
My body, the void.

Upon Arriving at Lake Maeji

> With the surface of the lake
> I likewise ripple out.
> Look, a mind
> uncircumscribed.

The Abyss of Sound

The steam whistle heard many years ago on the train from Kurye to Namwon. Permanently recorded, the sound still resounding somewhere in the vacant expanse of sky. That sound, so different from all the steam whistle sounds incessantly heard. That sound, as if it had eaten up the void-wraiths, as if it had eaten up the sky, so that it resonates emptiness; it's without a within. The sound which can not be regenerated even if each of the train passengers devotes three lifetimes to it. Even if all these minds and bodies are poured into it, unmoldable sound. Sound unkneadable even with all the tears and blood; and unpurchasable through thrift or squandering. The ungraspable steam whistle, even if the train should run for a thousand or ten thousand or countless days, ungraspable sound; the sound is also ungraspable with everything that is filled or hot, everything cold, everything that is clear or has a shape. Ungraspable sound. Intimate commerce with light years of space begets me in the gut of the void and I, in turn, in my belly carry the steam whistle sound. Pregnant with everything in the world, like the house of life and like a putrid hell.

Even now it resounds with an ear that communes with emptiness; at any rate, bottomless, limitless abyss—steam whistle sound!

Life-Mandala

Morning Glory
which I as a child had seen so much of
discloses morning
and begets dewdrops
echo of the morning sky
dew-suspended-flower mandala
mirrored in the beads of dew
a flower-of-eternal-reflection mandala
sanguine, the red dew's
echo, lifeblood in that
echo-mandala
dewdrops in
life in those beads of dew
flower in the eyeball
life-mandala.

While Blanketing the Earth
—I am Ant

Just because I say I'm Ant
doesn't mean I have all the virtues
ants possess.
I can
crawl.
I can be stepped on by anyone's foot.
While living in the ruins, I cannot be a ruin myself.
I could become a wasp waisted, black
tear drop the length of my own body,
and also while crawling, suddenly sprawled over,
be unable to right myself, laughing mindlessly.
I can wiggle through it,
my whole body straddling empty space,
the pseudo-death climax. That being the case,
how could even the sky not help being embraced by me
while blanketing the earth?

Looking into the Grass

I look into the clover
wanting to find
one with four leaves,
as I used to do in childhood.

What is the universe?
Looking into the grass.
What is Nirvana?
Looking into the grass.
What is salvation?
Looking into the grass.

Oh, looking into the grass
where a lucid glance discloses plenitude.

Fallen Leaves

Fallen leaves strewing the path
our foot steps traced
as if you purposely
effaced it, you indicate the path
so well that
you are the path.

Like Leaving Your Umbrella Behind

Unable to depart and leave me,
like an umbrella, behind, I
suffer.

If I leave myself behind,
all is sky,
all is love,
all is freedom.

As for the Body

As for the body
(apparently massive)
once lifted
it thereby renders itself
just wind.

Approaching another, irrespectively,
—in any case,
the body blows itself over
as if impact with a wall
blows it over.

0

. . . whither and whence from there to there
0 is the origin and end
0 is life's portrait
0 is the figuration of presence and absence empty and full
What is 0?
0 is light
the air's breathing
a roll and a game
a halo if donned
0 big and bright
0 is life's looking glass
0 is love
0, the meat of the grain
the flesh of the fruit
the soul of tears and dew
   of celestial bodies
   of rings of silver and gold
   of grass and of trees
   of water and blood
drops
a multiple of voices
a multiple of holes, their souls
death, its soul
0, its very soul.

Breath and Dream

Breath and Dream
—*On Poetry*

Chong Hyon-jong

As a poet, I think that it is quite improper to think about poetry. Poetry exists before we think about it—it comes before thought. We live in poetry and poetry lives in us without our thinking about it, just as a tree, without thinking about it, lives by means of air, sun, and water. Of course, the reading of poetry is no more of a passive process than the life of a tree. Reading is as much an active engagement as it is a passive assimilation. Insofar as reading is an act we perform, reading is active. At the same time, the fact that the act of reading evokes change lends it a passive quality. This is not to say that there is not a considerable amount of activity existing within the passivity of reading.

Just as nature and the universe belong to those who read its mysteries, poetry belongs to those who read it. Nature is a giant womb swarming with seeds and embryos, and poetry, too, is a womb and seed-ball in which we are born anew. All language is a ball of seeds, especially the language of poetry. That we are moved by poetry, that our feelings and consciousness are expanded by poetry as if we were pregnant—this is an indication that the space of poetry is pregnant, ready to give new birth to us. Poetry has been the matrix of new being from time immemorial, and the desire for rebirth has been one of the strongest desires of humankind. This desire is a dream which exists as long as we yearn for this life to be worth living and this world to be worth living in.

I stated above that it is improper to think about poetry, and this is because poetry is ever identical with itself, it is what it is. How can we express, then, the way in which we relate to poetry? Perhaps we can say that we do

113

not so much read poetry as breathe it. In my view, there is no other word to express the experience of poetry. While it is impossible to explain this assertion, I will attempt to shed some light on it.

Breath is one sure index of life; it is an axiom that all biological beings breathe. The breath I am discussing, however, is more than that—it is a metaphor which possesses a dimension of the mind as well as a dimension of society. In Korea, when we run into a difficulty or an obstacle, when find our lives burdensome, we say, *taptaphada, sum makhinda* (there is not enough air, we cannot breathe). When we have a brief spell of respite in the midst of a difficulty or emergency, we also say, *hansum tollinda* (now we can breathe) or *sumt'ongi naonda* (now the windpipe is open). We use these expressions at the moment of release from bodily tension, psychological coercion or social oppression, at the moment of escape from inner or outer constraint or at the moment we become free of a burden. The dancer leaps into the air and pauses momentarily at the apex of his or her leap and is thus released from gravity. As poetry breathes into us, our spirit leaps and soars, also released from our heaviness. While we can find similar movement in all other arts, poetry more than any other art allows us to experience a moment of liberation and openness. It is for this reason that I call poetry breath, the breath of liberation.

From a somewhat different perspective, breath is another symbol of life: vitality. There are times in the life of an individual or of a society when frustration and stagnation seem unavoidable. Our awareness and our senses become worn and unfeeling. While this dulling of the senses may conceal an unconscious desire to protect ourselves from harm, in view of the aspirations we have for ourselves in our lives, this represents a come-down, a let-down. Koreans say that "it is the dead fish that goes downstream, and it is the live fish that goes upstream." In *The Sorrows of Young Werther*, Goethe points out that what makes the world an evil place is not so much evil intentions as misunderstanding and habit. We can speak of death in both a factual and a metaphorical sense. We see death everywhere in the world on an everyday basis. We can say that just as there are deaths in fact, there are also metaphorical deaths in life. We are truly alive when our awareness and receptivity are fresh and keen. If this is the case, poetry is the breath which restores this freshness and keenness within us. Because it resists all that benumbs us, poetry is breath, the breath of life. Just as the wind is the breath of the universe, poetry, like wind, moves our spirit and opens us to life, becoming the ever-fresh source of life in the world. As breath, poetry becomes the force in our spirit, the rhythm which rises through our senses, heart, spirit, and body. Poetry is the space in which life is restored to the elemental self that has been crumpled and oppressed by civilization, institutions, and ideologies. Poetry is, therefore, breath, the breath of nature. When I assert that we do not read poetry but breathe it, these are some of the implications I attempt to invoke. These implications combine to make us realize that we do not simply breathe poetry—we live it.

We know that oxygen comes from trees. Where does the breath of poetry come from? Dreams. It comes from dreams. The Korean word for dream is *kkum*, a word which in addition to signifying the dreams of sleep, wishes, ambitions, also points to what is imagined, daydreamed, yearned for, and seen in visions. The meaning of *kkum* depends on the context in which it is used. In any case, there are few words that have thicker layers of meaning than the word *kkum*.

When I consider my own work, I find that I have been making use of this word quite frequently. About ten years ago, I began writing a sequence of poems under the overall title of *The Dream of Things*. Following this, I wrote essays on the subject suggested by the title. My belief at the time was that the dream of things was also my dream. I believed that the objects of my poetry—a tree, a political event, the virtues of the spirit—were things which came into poetry to realize their dreams through me. It is said that it was the habit of a certain traditional Chinese artist, when he wanted to paint, let us say, a tree, to try to become that tree, to look at it until he became it. (Seeing, looking, contemplating, this is, either with Eastern masters of meditation or Western mystics, an important method of arriving at the truth, of coming face to face with the numen.) This, what the painter tried to accomplish, was an impossibility. If I become a tree, I cannot paint it. It is sad, it is tragic, I said to myself, that I cannot become a tree. But poetry is born in the moment of this estrangement. If I cannot become a tree in the world of facts, however, I can become a tree in the world of analogies. The world of poetry is the world of analogy. The space of poetry is where I can be a tree and at the same time remain myself. In other words, the I and the non-I, this and that, the things that differ from each other, can be, in the space of poetry, their own selves and other than their own selves. It is for this reason that poetry is the bridge which connects art and history, man and nature, the sacred and the profane.

It is the dream or imagination which coalesces things in this manner. The imagination acquires a body in our bodies and the dream acquires a body in reality. The dream has its own history; it is beautiful because it draws substance from history or its absence. This is the ironic make-up of the life we live.

The Korean poet Han Yongun (1879-1944) wrote a poem entitled "The Silence of Love":

Love is gone. Ah, my love is gone.
Sundering the mountain's green color,
   severing our ties, love is gone
   down a path leading to a maple
   grove.
The old vows, firm and glowing like a gold
   blossom, have turned to cold dust and
   flown away in the breeze of a sigh.
The memory of a keen first kiss reversed the
   compass needle of my fate, then retreated
   and vanished.
I am deafened by love's fragrant words and
   blinded by love's blossoming face.
Love, too, is a man's affair. We feared
   parting at meeting, warned against it,
   but parting came unawares and the startled
   heart bursts with new sorrow.
Yet I know that to make parting the source of
   vain tears is to sunder myself my love, so
   I transformed the unruly power of sorrow
   and poured it over the vertex of new hope.
As we fear parting when we meet, so we
   believe we will meet again when we part.
Ah, my love is gone, but I have not sent my
   love away.
My song of love whose melody cannot endure
   itself curls around the silence of love.[1]

We should pay particular attention to the last line: "My song of love whose melody cannot endure itself curls around the silence of love." Love is, but is silent. Consequently, we cannot hear or see love. Love, the beloved, is that which should be present but is absent: that which should be fullness is now only a lack. And yet it is the inability to hear or see love, our beloved, the absence of what should be present, which makes the poet's song of love overflow the lack and curl around it. At the same time, the poet believes that he will be seeing his love face to face in the future. This belief is grounded in the song of love that curls around the silence of love, in other words, in the poet's dream that the void will be filled.

[1] Translated by Peter H. Lee.

The dream is motion and action. Poetry is the art, the spell, of invoking the beloved, of bridging the beloved's absence, of building a road between being and non-being. The dream of poetry gives birth to breath, which, in turn, blows into the spirit of whoever hears the poet—the breath of this dream invites one to take part in the process of embodiment, of incarnation. Although we can consider this the process of sharing in the passion of absence, the moment we are with poetry we feel the pain of individuation disappear and joy swell up in this sharing. This is precisely the meaning of music and dance which Nietzsche tried to share with us.

Life is the tension between what is and what should be. Paradoxically, what should be comes from what is. The moment there is a perception of what is as it really is, what should be begins to stir, to move, to be born. If we keep in mind what I have discussed above as the dream of things, we see that dreams obtain justification and embodiment only when they are rooted in the concrete objects of the world and in history. The dream, therefore, is a space in between what is and what should be. When we say that poetry is the fruit of a dream, then, we are also saying that it is a space of movement and fusion occurring between what is and what should be.

Lack is suffering; fullness is joy. Life and history give us pain because of lack, but this lack is what makes dreams and what makes songs. It is here where the greatness of the song comes in. We are poor, but our song need not be poor. Our song may be about sorrow, but it satisfies the dream of sorrow and gives us the peace of fulfilled joy as long as it remains a song.

All acts of creation are difficult, and writing poetry is a difficult and painful task. Pain comes when the dream of things enters us and desires to become our dream. When we long for freedom, for peace, for love, for justice, and the poet sings of this longing, the poet must him or herself be freedom, love, peace, justice. For the poet, then, poetry is suffering. This is because I cannot be what I sing. In other words, poetry is where contradictions and conflicts clash and also where they reach out for reconciliation; it is where this and that, what is and what should be, come together in clashes and in reconciliation. Clashing is pain: reconciliation is joy. The pain of the poet is indeed a strange joy.

The world and history are a continuous postponement of our dream, a continuous projection of our dream into futurity, but poetry grants us moments of blessedness and restores our present to us.

Translated by Uchang Kim and Ted Hughes

117

CORNELL EAST ASIA SERIES

FORTHCOMING

To order, please contact the Cornell East Asia Series, East Asia Program, Cornell University, 140 Uris Hall, Ithaca, NY 14853-7601, USA; phone (607) 255-6222, fax (607) 255-1388, internet: er26@cornell.edu, http://www.einaudi.cornell.edu/eastasia/EastAsiaSeries.html.

3-98/1.2M pb/.3M hc/BB